To Wyatt and Kira (...and all of the snails in our yard.)

In memory of my second grade teacher, Mrs. Jacobson.
Thank you for always being one of my biggest fans.
You were a truly special person.

Copyright © 2020 by Robyn Bowman. Cover/Illustrations copyright © by Robyn Bowman. All rights reserved. Published by RB Publishing. No part of this book may be reproduced or transmitted in any form or by any means, electronic or mechanical, including photocopying, recording, or by any information storage and retrieval system, without written permission from the publisher.

First edition, October 2020

ISBN 978-1-73576-740-6

The illustrations were created digitally using Procreate.
The text is set in 32 pt Chaloops.

www.robynbowman.com

The (kinda boring, not that great, PRETTY SUPER AWESOME) Garden Snail

By Robyn Bowman

Oh hi! It's me, Snail. I'm not like most creatures. Soon you will find I have quite interesting features.

A **SNAIL**? No way!
It cannot be true!

But I can hide under this leaf and **NO ONE** will see.

The size of a hippo's teeth may be **greater**.

But I have more teeth than **175** alligators!

14,000 teeny tiny teeth, to be exact! I sure hope the Tooth Fairy has a big piggy bank! He-he-he.

Give me some veggies.
I will eat them **all day**.

I'll **never** beat a cheetah.
They run far too **fast**.

But in a race with a sloth, honestly, I'll still come in **LAST**.

I'm never going to beat this sloth! I'm the world's slooooooowest moving animal. SIGH.

A bouncy kangaroo can jump over **FIVE** tires.

Just give me a wall and I will climb **even higher!**

I'm not like a cat,
I can **barely** see.

But I can smell that garden over there... did you plant it just for ME?!

I think I'll have a salad today.

I'll **never** be soft, fluffy, fuzzy or fine.

But that trail behind me is made of **PURE SLIME!!**

Fly south for the winter?
That's **NOT** for me.

With my house on my back,
I'm as **happy** as can be.

I can't swing like a monkey because arms I am **lacking**.

But I have **one big foot**, and it's great for backpacking!

It looks like it might be my tummy, but it's actually my foot!

I'm not like a puppy who eats lots of **kibble**.

So if you find me in your garden, please don't be mad if I **nibble**.

And if you're like most kids who love **splashing** in the rain...

PLEASE watch where you're stomping, or I could experience some **PAIN!!!**

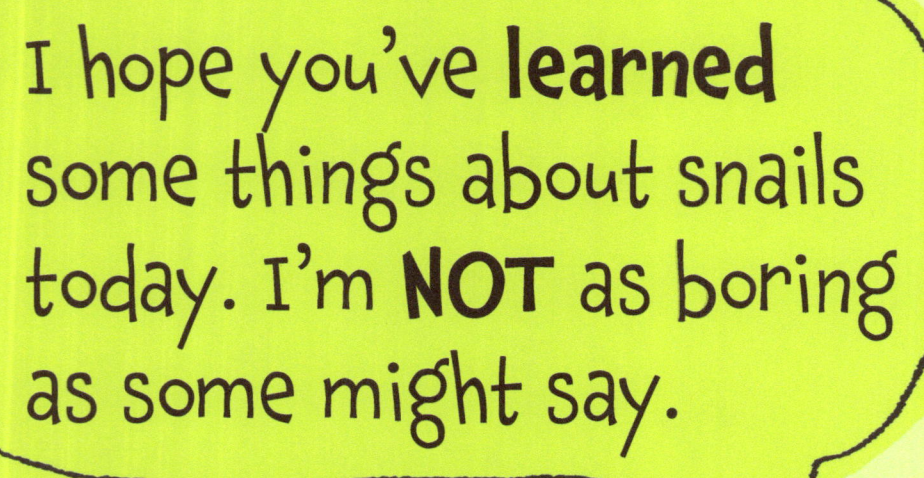

So the next time you see that slimy trail, remember...

I'm pretty **SUPER AWESOME**...for a tiny garden snail.

www.ingramcontent.com/pod-product-compliance
Lightning Source LLC
Chambersburg PA
CBHW042255100526
44589CB00002B/31